Thoughts
of a
Daydreamer

A Simple Book of Poems

MARK A. KLEIN

Balboa Press books may be ordered through booksellers or by contacting:

Balboa Press
A Division of Hay House
1663 Liberty Drive
Bloomington, IN 47403
www.balboapress.com
844-682-1282

ISBN: 978-1-9822-5833-7 (sc)
ISBN: 978-1-9822-5834-4 (e)

Library of Congress Control Number: 2020922134

Print information available on the last page.

Balboa Press rev. date: 11/19/2020

BALBOA.PRESS

Contents

In Search of Love

A Spiritual Place

Life is a Journey

Darker Paths

A Blessed Family

In Search of Love

I think of you

In the silence of the night I think of you
As if to feel the warmth of your smile
A gentle stare, the love you have for me
Your visit gives comfort to my soul

Such a delight is your presence
Memories flow like rushing streams
Living not dead, Spirit not form
Immersed in love

In eternities unending peace
Shall we rejoice
That souls unite once again
And this sadness be no more

What we were missing

As I look back at a time gone by
Way before my years in Junior High
I can't recall exactly when
Our paths first briefly crossed

We weren't real close as friends you know
But I always seemed to like you though
That when I heard you were in town
I had to come and see you

Your face was to my grand delight
So young and smiling, a beautiful site
I hoped in your heart that you just might
Think I was handsome too

We seemed to find attraction there
And since have made this quite a fair
Growing in each other's care
More every day that passes

I never dreamt of a time or day
Your eyes would somehow turn my way
And lead me to that better place
To find what we were missing

We've made a pledge to see this through
And hope that it will blossom into
The love we both have longed for
In our hearts

So, take this next big step with me
And forever may we always be
A joy for all the world to see
Our hearts desire to one another

Remember This

I want to tell my wife today
That love has surely come my way
That I will always cherish her
And thank the Lord I married her

Children we have had together
A faith that withstands any weather
I always know my place is with her
And when I'm far away I miss her

Let her please remember this
That I will love her everyday
My heart she sure has stole away
For God has made us blessed as one
Until our time on earth is done

Our Dance

Your hand in mine clinched tight
My cheek upon your hair
Our bodies pressed as we unite
While others softly stare

With grace we sway across the floor
The rhythm carries us away
You glance at me and I smile back
Nowhere else we'd rather be

I sing softly in your ear
Consumed in pure delight
Hoping this dance does not end here
Nor by mornings early light

Beauty from Within You

Your eyes proceed you like a beacon in a crowd
They lead as you saunter through
The focus is upon you the stir begins
Your bold beauty stands unharnessed

They become impatient to draw you near
Joy is released I see their faces
Honesty and passion flow freely from within you
It penetrates thickest skin

The warmth that you bring to every encounter
Gives feelings of happiness too hard to contain
What words can describe such dominant a force
Such fullness of life that would serve you justice

Only beauty such as yours can shine quite this bright
And grace all of those who stand in your light
May you never take lightly this gift that you give
That makes better a place this world that we live

Blossom Waiting Still

Blossom of thy heart yearning to unleash
Trapped in mortal fear the pain of true belief
There holds the truth untold where none can so reveal
Into the depths it drowns no chance of sight or feel

Escape the depths it will when time is right perhaps
To meet the one with whom my yearning heart entraps
I shall not see the wake or predetermine when
As time thus only knows for whence the bud begins

For when the wait is o'er, and light has shown thy path
The blossom shall unfold, and you'll be in its grasp
For size will only tell of your intent returned
For you will be the one I have forever yearned

The Smile of an Angel

I see the light in your eyes, your hair and your smile
That brightens my day without choice of my own
That soothes my surroundings
And warms all my senses

I see joy in your presence, your step and your manner
A magnet of magnitude that tugs at my heart
That pulls at my chest
Draws me close

I see beauty and elegance that can't be contained
That's beyond your control
As deep as the center of your soul

I see love without particular aim
Without boundaries of space
Emanating its presence on all in our presence

I see strength, in your character, your grip and your voice
A confidence of self and pride of one's own
The weight that you bear
Seems light to your touch

You surrounded me without even a step
Captured my thoughts without saying a word
Entered my self without the touch of your hand

What else would you be but graced by God
A heart of an Angel and full of God's Love

Never

I never met a woman quite like you
or ever had a dream like this come true

Bits and pieces falling into place
Like the perfect formation of time and space

Never saw it coming, just prayed it would
Never imagined life with someone could be this good

I'll never need or want for this again
For a love like this shall never end

Always with me

I know we don't see each other very often
But I know you are there
Because I can feel you are with me
You are a part of me and always will be

I know you pray for me often
And that gives me comfort
I think about you often
And wish I could hear your voice

I pray for you and hope you are happy
I don't want you to think I have forgotten you
Because I have not, and won't
I just wanted you to know I love you
Always….

Making Memories

There's time in the present
There's time in the past
But, it's the time in the future
Where memories will last

May the Memories we've started
The Memories to come
The Memories we'll share
Be the most amazing ones

Together we'll be, as this time passes by
Your Husband…...My Wife
Are how the Memories we'll make
Mark the rest of our life

Till Then

No waiver does my heart impart
For you have won me from the start

Should you return your heart to me
How happy the both of us would be

Till that day comes where we unite
I'll gaze upon these sleepless nights

Without You

Will there ever be a day
When you can't get me off your mind
When you need me as much as I need you
I hope the sun doesn't rise in the morning
Or set again at night
When I do not have you with me
But time slips slowly past the horizon
And again, I find myself alone

Your Smiling Face

Your eyes pierce softly through squinted lash
With cheeks raised high the dimples flash
The pearly whites light up your face
Through golden skin, the suns embrace

Your lips entice with softest shine
The color of a sweet red wine
Your long blonde hair falls right in place
A reflection of angelic grace

Your gaze reflects my souls delight
I kiss your cheek you hold me tight
This happy I may never be
Without your face smiling back at me

Wedding Day

Tick Tock, the clock chimes toll
Let your wedding day start to unfold
Your dress is laid out
The Brides Maids all chosen
The Groom is quite nervous
His toes are all frozen
Both families have blessed
that you should unite
You'll saunter down the aisle
without any fight
The rings will be placed
on your hands with such care
With the smell of fresh flowers
softly floating in the air
The vows will be said
The couple made one
Gods Blessings bestowed on you
Let the Church bells be rung

Light of my Life

My Lovely Bride
Means so much to me
Without her love
I don't know where I'd be

The Sun wouldn't shine
The Stars would not sparkle
My dreams not complete
Nor my thoughts near as thoughtful

But the stars are full of light
And my thoughts are always bright
She is the reason
I sleep at peace through the dark of the night

A Spiritual Place

Let the rain come down

Let the rain come down
Baptize me with water
No one was involved
It came straight from the father

I ask him to forgive me
Release me from my sin
Without any hesitation
He let the rain come down

My heart filled with joy
And I ran through the rain
I burst out in laughter
It was like I felt no more pain

I feel like I don't deserve it
For all the things that I've done
But he looked in my heart
And he let the rain come down

He did not need any churches
To recognize what he'd done
He saved me once and for all
When he let that rain come down

Everlasting
I can live forever

So, what is my hurry
Cherish the moment I am in
Peace is all around me
The holy spirit fills my soul

I feel my body
but the spirit knows no pain
There is strain on my heart
but the heart beats on

My mind is heavy.
But my spirit is light
Secom to the spirit
Let me enter into its peace

No enemy can defeat the spirit
For it is everlasting
Surrender the mind
Let it not impede the way

Peace lies in the spirit
Let it carry me
Become one with it
So, I too am everlasting

Having Faith

Why do I always think of bad
When thinking of things, I've never had
I've always had the things I need
By faith in God I still succeed

I challenged the things I didn't like
But time has shown, he's always right
So, why do I fear what the future holds
For what's in store God only knows

It's made me strong; it's made me see
That God has lots of love for me
For the story book that reads my name
Is not a tale to be ashamed

A humble son is what I'll be
And thank the Lord for being me

By Your Grace

Oh, Lord my God, be with me today
In everything I do and say
Everywhere and every place
Let my heart be full of grace

Let your mercy flow from me
For all the doubting world to see
For I can be a shining light
To triumph o'er the darkest knight

With saints of old to lead my path
And you to fend me from Hell's wrath
I shall not fear my journey's end
But, know you've freed me from my sin

So, let me meet this day with faith
Knowing you have saved me by your grace

Always brings us back to you

Please my God I pray today
The sights and sounds I hear this day
Will meld my heart to act a way
That guides my fellow may to stay
In touch with you both night and day

Your gift of scripture is a grace
A blessing that we should embrace
The stories that you have to tell
Is our true guide for living well

So, if we tend to go astray
Lives that seem so in dismay
Families, friends and scriptures too
Shall always bring us back to you

Bible and Beer

I recall the day I bought a Bible and some beer
I really needed to cry, but found no tear
It was all balled up inside me and I needed to get it out.
Maybe it was time to see what God was all about

I messaged my kids, but got no reply
I messaged some old friends. Just to say hi.
I couldn't find the answers I needed anywhere.
So, I sat down with that new bible
in my old rocking chair

The passages were old. But, seemed to make sense.
Some about evil. And some about recompense.
It started to provide me with answers I'd long sought.
Made a lot of sense about what Mom and Daddy taught.

It's been a while now, and I'm still hangin on.
Mending broken fences along the way
So, if you want to find me. Well I'll be right here
Hangin on to this old bible, Drinkin this cold beer

Strength for a Day

Let me have the strength today
To conquer challenges passed my way
To have the foresight on my side
That shows the wisdom deep inside

To always make the Godly choices
And disallow those other voices
Let me know the right from wrong
And have the courage to stay strong

The Way

Face today and face tomorrow
With a whole lotta hope
And not full of sorrow

The beginning is now
Lay the pain at the door
Shoot for the stars
And a whole lot more

Your spirit is strong
Your faith will not cower
Cause Peace is the way
And God has the power

Forgiveness

That of the past that you wish forgotten is forgotten
No burden shall lay heavy upon thine heart

For it is God's will that a man should forgive thy neighbor
Not with ties or stipulations should it impose

Free from mind never to reside again
Waste not this precious gift

This Wood
A Walking Stick

This is no ordinary Wood.
But, rather a reminder of life and transformation.
A life that was strong and vibrant.
But, as life changed and time took its toll. Became weak and dying.
But, even in its worst state was noticed for it's potential.
Now This Wood has regained new life and new meaning.

This Wood represents a journey.
A life almost lost, now found.
And a new path to follow.

This Wood was splintered from the stress.
Now it is mended.
Representing its strength to overcome

This Wood is stained.
Not to cover up its marks of life.
But, rather to highlight its imperfections uniting them in a pattern of beauty and luster.

This Wood is now made whole.
With personal notes of a life worth living.
Loved by many.

May This Wood lead you down many a path.
And however steep or winding or treacherous.
May This Wood keep you steady and safe though all of your journeys.

And, may This Wood be a reminder of your strength and ability to overcome.

Life is a Journey

Trapped in a one-sided story

Truths untold and swept away
Never to see the light of day
A shadow cast on misguided youth
Oh, how to unveil that untold truth

The years slip by, no chances had
To tell your story of how it all went bad
The recollections didn't seem so sad
Lost in perceptions of dear ol' dad

I pray a day to set things right
If ever a day could be so bright
A dream I've had since this began
To become the dad, I know they always had

To set things straight
Since much time has past
Won't bring back lost days
For that pain shall always last

Paradise lies at no man's feet

Until earth washes away
And flesh is no more
Struggle and strife
Make up an honest man's life

Easy has no place here
Pain and fear seem so clear
Relentless sometimes it seems
Thin lines drawn between reality and dreams

The struggle seems a daunting task
How much longer the man will often ask
And as he puts the memories behind him
A sharp reminder seems to find him

Nothing easy lays before us
Not worth having if it did
Proud the man who meets the task
And wavers not against the strain

For in the end when paradise is near
The fear will fade, and pain melt away
For his head will lift high
Knowing that life has not beat him
And that he has not lived in vain

My Fairy Tale

There is no fairy tale
No fairy tale for me
If there were a fairy tale in sight
Dare I think that it be for me

Not at once nor not at all
No princess in a tower tall
No kiss awaits a sleepy bride
Or steed of white for me to ride

No maiden claimed to be so fair
With locks of long and flowing hair
Not even a stolen pot o' gold
Or tarnished lamp for me to hold

But wish I may and wish I might
On a shining star cast in the night
That you yourself would wish upon
Where fairy tales come true

Daydreams

The time of day the hour it seems
An eternity cast in long daydreams
The wishes great, the wishes small
The dreams in which include them all

If interruptions didn't come
And ends to dreams would never come
What fate would lie in those conclusions
So vast and mystic these illusions

Would happiness always prevail
Or darkness have its tale to tell
Let's hope we never see the day
When all daydreams just go away

Much to Tell

I could have much to verse about
and tell with all my heart
To share of me what's known by few
and only mine to see

Why must I not talk of home
or memories of yesteryear
If done with sparing choice
that few will ever hear

I'd think it prime to be the one
who's chosen when it's time
For if the interest is only mine
I'll bury deep within

And cherish with mine own accord
till I or it should fade
No further versed in word
or future attention paid

In my Dementia

Where does the mind wait
Until our human form is done
And our immortality takes over

Where are my thoughts
Are they really mine
Patience is a virtue
But is escapes me

Time is not real
I'm lost in this space
Do I have a name
Since this is not me

Remember what I was
Not what I have become
I'll know you again
And I'll wait for you

Searching

Do you search for some unknown self
Unrecognized as the mirror stares back
As if searching for a lost child
Not resembling what once was

An inner being playful with eyes wide open
Looking upon the earth with no fear
somehow misplaced or stolen by circumstance
Waiting to be found and renewed to former self

To once again look upon a new day
With peace of heart that is one's self
Recognized by only you refreshed in spirit
with a vibrance for life

So Many Friends

I don't know how it started
Or ever came to be
The friendships of so many years
Still bless my life you see

We stay in touch and still hang out
Whenever we get the chance
And then to say goodbye again
With a hug or fleeting glance

I know we'll never really part
Or loose this feeling in our hearts
For true friends we will ever be
Bonds that tie them all to me

We will remain

If I die tomorrow
Don't doubt that you are loved
There's no need to search forgiveness
There is nothing to forgive

I have no true regrets
My life has been amazing
Beyond my wildest dreams
From the valleys to the peaks

Of course, there have been disappointments
Who has lived if that weren't true
My heart has been broken
I realized I did not know what I was looking for

I've had happiness, true happiness
All out there in love
I wish this upon all of you
Friend or foe just one this much
Loved more than deserved

Is this the end, not for me
Can't fathom what it's like
My only wish is that I know you
That we don't end, ever
Only goodness remains, we remain

In my Memory

I am a Repository
One after another old-time story
All living in their time of glory
There is something special about them all

Some are family and some are friends
Some are just people I ran into now and again
But they are still alive and doing well
And in my memory is where they dwell

I'll tell their story till the day I die
Then I'll join them living up on high
I hope our story will carry on
But, in Your Memory, living strong

They did not know Her

Went to a funeral today
An old friend who passed away
Pastor's words seemed strange must say
The words of the eulogy they pray
"All the friends say", was a common theme
Not, "I knew her" or "she once said"
But, "I was told she was so"
Because they did not really know her

She drew membership through her works
And she was active in the church
Sunday school she led
The book of God to them she read
She was a beautiful soul they said
Yet they did not know her
No, they did not know her

Seems strange to me
How distant they seemed to be
Seems as if they did not know her

True Wealth

Take the time to know yourself
Take the time to know true wealth
The time is not in the wealth you spend
The wealth is in the time you spend

Take care not to lose it all
But, take the care to make the hall
To last the temps that temp the fate
To find the love for all who waits

For all is none and one is all
The love that cushions when you fall
To live the dream that hates to wait
Be not the one to hesitate

So, take the time and make the best
For true the love that pass the test
Truth be known to all the bold
Life's manifest to you unfold

Take ripe the fruit upon the vine
And chose the one whose heart be thine

A Lonely Farewell

Tis the time for longing
The time for pain
A gap within my heart
Where no one can explain

I've tried forgetting
But memories still prevail
Thought I could make it happen
But I fear I've lost too much

You've distanced yourself from me
I try to understand. I search for reason
No matter the explanation I give myself
The pain does not subside

Maybe I'm better off that you let me go
Maybe I did not try hard enough
Why won't you see me
Maybe it is too hard on you

Or maybe You have had enough
I probably will never know
We are different in so many ways
But, so familiar in just as many

You tantalize my being
Another I will not find
You tease me and then break away
I think this hurts the most

I want to see you, if only for the last time
It's not as if I have died
and no one can reach me
I am here, waiting, longing, void

Take away that I still love you
The way we part is no comfort
You are so special
We're more different than maybe I can see

Friendship, love or maybe nothing
Where will we go
If you'll have none of me
and wish me farewell

I guess I must move on
But, know this, it is not a simple thing
I did not take it lightly when I said I love you
My heart is with you

Though I doubt yours is of mine
Peace and happiness be all your days
For I shall not forget
No, I shall not forget

Silence to Sleep

Have you listened to the silence
As you lay alone in bed
Only thoughts of gentle humming
Filling up an empty head

No dancing little sugar plums
Or sheep to count to sleep
Nothing but the silent dark
As you drift away to sleep

Coming To

The breaths are short
I cannot get enough
I feel I am choking
What is this on my neck?
What is this in my nose?
Now I know where I am at
But almost at the point of panic
I still can't catch my breath
The guy, he tries to calm me
I keep my fear at bay
Now I feel the pain
The night has just begun

Broken Cough

Like knives that pierce my side
Each cough brings on the pain
I can feel the bones shift
Catching me off guard

Clinching my teeth together
A moan comes from my throat
I grasp firmly at my side
Damn, here it comes again

Down Deep

There's a place down deep inside
I swore I'd always hide
That holds the deepest yearnings of my heart

The lock upon its hasp
Is far from the normal grasp
That I can barely reach that depth at all

To share what's kept within
Could unleash a bitter end
Or release things I'm not used to

Looking Back

I want to tell you about it all
The now, the when, the after all
The time I spent just growing older
Upward, wiser, a little bolder

It feels so good to look back when
I like to do it now and then
I had it all, not always right
Finished well, put up a fight

The drinks, the laughter with my friends
That always start with "remember when"
It's made me who I am today
I know that's why I feel this way

My Poetry

I don't understand this poet's rhyme
The words she used to set the time
To help me understand this thing
Some new language from me must spring

The thoughts, the words, I do not grasp
My English Teacher would be a gas
My interest in this special verse
Is strange to me but not a curse

Mine come to me at the strangest times
The words, the verse, the simple rhymes
A little voice whispers in my ear
The purpose really isn't very clear

So, why do I write this poetry
I guess I will just have to wait and see

Darker Paths

Dark Places

In darkest places where most folks won't go
You will find me
Not because I am lost
But because I am looking for others

Friends who have steered the wrong path
Or those just in search of a friend
It is a lonely place
For I have almost taken those wrong turns

So, I live on the edge of that place
Just at an arm's length
Close enough to grab an outstretched hand
And pull them to the other side

If you have never been there
You should go
To gain an understanding for what you have
And to know what your friends are going through

Moving On

The thoughts become struggles
The absence of a place called home
My roots have been sniped from the depth
No longer to grow here

Always new, always beginnings
So unsettled a life of unrest
My place is unknown
For where shall I land

I yearn so to sit down
To plant and harvest a crop of my own
Land with familiar footsteps
For I have traveled here so many times

For what do I leave but swirls of dry dust
Some better, some worse or no change at all
Do hallowed halls still echo my name
Or recollect my existence at all

Will this one be it, I look to the road
What memories await, Unfold as they will
Hesitant but anxious, ready but wait
As torn from my peel, never to be the same

What else but to trust
This dream of that place
The time, how soon
How much more must I wait

I go on so much further
Always checking to the rear
Only time will define me
With patience, I move on

In Hard Times

My God, My God I call to you
I call to you in times so blue
This hollow feeling spans my chest
Are you present, why must I jest

For you would never leave me here
Alone to face my naked fear
I need to feel you here with me
To give me strength, to help me see

To see the grandeur of your plan
Is bigger that one single man
That in my eyes what may seem wrong
Is what I need to make me strong

Sometimes this life, it hurts so bad
The times we wish we never had
So, let me feel your warm embrace
And fill me with your gentle grace

That I can see things once again
Through happy eyes, a gentle grin
I have a faith in you alone
Please let this prayer to you be known

Gentle Hush

Have you ever seen the trees
The spiders and the bumble bees
The hummingbird with songs of glee
Spreads their wings and fly so free

I watch the living of the earth
And wonder of their untamed birth
How nature helps them to survive
To live in peace, such gentle lives

The wondrous things we fail to see
As life drifts by for you and me
Don't let it pass in such a rush
Just stop and feel the gentle hush

Journey's End

Oh, my back my head my hands
Dripping sweat, burning sand
I work so hard to stay alive
I wonder if I will survive

The sun keeps beating down on me
My vision blurs, I can barely see
Straight ahead my path doth lead
Buzzards waiting for a feed

I think I see some water there
Run I must to get my share
Falling flat into the sand
So, this is where my journey ends

Stories End

The tales of love they torture my heart
For without thee I am but hollow
And time move not fast enough
When the void is filled with joy
For stories end is what I long
The love I search waits for me there

Vanish

I listen to silence
More than I listen to sound
I pray to the heavens
Yet unsure where I'm bound
I see no one around me
'less I venture to town
Could vanish without warning
And not expect to be found

Feeling Inside

I don't know what I'm feeling
I just know it's not right
The prison walls surround me
Every day and every night

In my dreams and when awake
Tears at my body and blurs all my sight
I'm lost for a reason
Not sure what to blame

Is my course in misdirection
Does this failing have a name
Will it ever come together
I guess God only knows

All questions without answer
Pounding in my brain

Lost

There are lights in the distance
Swinging left to right
Dogs barking loudly
As if searching in the night

A little girl is missing
APB has been announced
Misdirected and searching
I call out, but no answer

I can see her right there!
But she is not looking back
Her head has turned from me
Filled with anger and hurt

I feel she wants me
But the influence is too strong
Her mother's twisted spirit
Stands shadowing the path

Will I ever see her again
Most important, will she ever see me
Does she even know she is lost
Or, has her memory faded

Will I be around to greet her
if she ever does come back
Or has the hurt grown to deep
Sad…... but true story

Real to me

And, my lost little girl

Why

On a day when the summer sun
Set high up in the sky
A mother feels the loss of her beloved son
She looks up at heaven on high
And asks the good Lord
Why Why Why

As his children hear the painful news
That their Daddy won't be coming home
And all the things he's not gonna see them do
They wonder why he was taken so soon
Confused about their bedtime prayers
Why Why Why

His Wife and friend of fifteen years
Is drowning in a pool of tears
While screaming out her greatest fears
All the dreams are shattered and
now her body trembles

She wonders how she'll carry on
So much work's been left undone
Her face pressed in her pillow crying
Why Why Why

We can't comprehend the Lord's great plan
Through the eyes of such a simple man
Fighting for our freedom
The sacrifice was always near

As he faced his greatest fear but still went on
He fought for those he's left behind
For causes so unclear, he asked
Why Why Why

Until we cross through heaven's gate
We'll never know what fate awaits
We will all be asking
Why Why Why

For Time to Pass

'Tis thine eye should secret hold
For that of mind be left untold
That in the darkest channels there
Be pain and grief alone despair

To glimpse of better day ahead
A line so fine should bleakness tread
To wish for time to move along
For renders in a happier song

A distance from a dreaded past
The chance again to breath at last
So, secret shall not ever leave
How some forever I should grieve

But if it should consume me not
Regain some joyous cheerful thought
Replace the dark and deep despair
For pleasant dreams await somewhere

Eternal Demise

Deep inside my heart
I know I am good
I was raised by my Granny
Who to me was a Saint

My world around me as of late is dark
Anger and hate have filled my heart
My limits have been reached
She has now pushed me too far

I fear for the sake of others
Of what I am capable of
Oh Lord please help your weary child
For a life I can't take if I am to be by your side

By: Torrie W. Klein

A Blessed Family

My Little Man

When I look at you, I'm in such awe
To see a child that has no flaw
For in my eyes you are so right
A child that's mine is such a sight

That God would bless your Mom and Me
With a gift for all the world to see
For I will do the best I can
To raise you as a fine young man

With dreams to set the world a fire
And the drive to make them all transpire
For I'll be with you through it all
And catch you if you ever fall

You'll make me proud; I know it's true
Cause I'm so proud just having you
I'll be your biggest fan
And you'll always be My Little Man

This Much More

Wiggly squiggly bouncy fun
I've just gained another son
What a joy, Oh what a laugh
It feels so good to have another
I'm just as proud as of the other

Your so cute and I'm so proud
I'd like to scream out in a crowd
How God could bless your Mom and Me
This much more, I cannot see

I will love you every day
And, wash your hurt and fears away
I promise you a part of me
For your Dad I'll always be

So, let's go out and have some fun
To celebrate the birth of my new son

A Dream Come True

A hope, a wish, a dream come true
I've prayed for a little girl like you
For all the world's riches can't compete
To our family you've made complete

For where would I be without you here
To fill my heart up with great cheer
So, take this pledge to you I give
To make this place for you to live

A better place where dreams come true
Where love and hope are near to you
Where you may know the Lord on high
And where we leave you room to fly

May all life's beauty you behold
May all life's wonders to you unfold
For all you try, you'll have no fear
Just knowing that your Dad is here

Your Brothers and your Mom and me
Could not be happier for you to be
A part of all we plan to see
As one big happy family

Daddy's Little Girl

A young little girl
With bright hazel eyes
Glimmering brown hair
A little long for her size

Full of wishes and dreams
Not the tom girl she seemed
But, bound to be a Daddy's girl
To shine a light on his whole world

He'd pick her up when she fell down
Tried real hard not to let her frown
Her every want he tried to please
Which for him came with such ease

As time would pass and they got older
The laughs and jokes were that much bolder
A bond would grow so strong and true
That nothing could ever part the two

She married and had kids of her own
A struggle of which she'd never known
And to her rescue he would fly
And put some light back in her eye

So, when time came 'twas her turn to be
The one to care for him you see
And though the part it sadly came
Their love for each other will forever remain

Haley's Comet

Sitting, watching from afar
As if we've seen a shooting star
The way you sing and play guitar
Let's us know that you'll go far

How far you ask? Well let us see
Just how big can big dreams be
As big as the Atlantic ocean
Only when you get the notion

As big as stars are in the sky
Why sure! We see it in your eye
You've got the gift, you've got the style
All the things that make us smile

Live your dream as big as you want it
Just take the ride on Hailey's Comet!

My Brothers

Can you believe how time has flown
Just yesterday it seems I was back at home
I recall the times, the good and bad
and wonder what I never had

I always had a place to stay
And yet I chose to go away
To school, to work, to travel about
To learn real quick to do without

A lot of friends have come and gone
And yet I still can carry on
I thank the Lord each and every day
For those who made me strong this way

The little things you did and said
Embedded in my thick ol' head
No drugs, no wrong,
keep my faith and keep it strong

We never talked enough to say
All the things us boys don't say
But I can't go another day
Not saying what I need to say

My life would not have turned out this way
Without the love and support you always gave
If I had to do it all again
I wouldn't change a dog-gone thing

So, without any further delay
I'll tell you what I want to say
That God has blessed my life this way
And I love you more than words say

Your Baby Brother

My Grandma

A dear sweetheart you were to sit me
A pain of a child I know I had to be

The times we had I never will forget
The joy I felt, I'm feeling even yet

The lord above has blessed the likes of you
And because of you, I know he's blessed me too

For you have always hoped and prayed for me
And my Grandma is what you'll always be

A Letter to Dad

I wonder some time if you can still think of me
Or if you ever had thoughts of
what you wanted me to be
The Father I lost or was taken from me
That I never knew but wanted to be

I wish you were still here so I could talk to you
To ask you for guidance on what I should do
My life has been rough without you to lead
To fill that basic Father Son need

I've learned what I had to by watching others
The best guides I had were my own older brothers
I know that you spent more time with them than me
Therefore, their example has helped me to see
Of what it would be like to have you around
An image of you that maybe I'd found

I feel that you were too busy with others
And I will never know you like all of my brothers
I do not remember you saying that you loved me
Only one short hug exists in my memory

I know you were good, so many people tell
But I have a hard time remembering that very well
There are so many things I wish you'd have seen
To coach me along through my years as a teen
Even my football games and my college grad
Every time I think of it, it makes me quite sad.

I know it's not your fault that God took you so soon
But he has sent others to keep me in tune
I am proud you are my Dad and
the things that you did
Now a lot of time has passed since I was a kid

I wish I could have really known
the great father of mine
And oh, so hope we can reunite
when God calls my time

I love you and miss you father

Mother you will always be

You've loved me since the day I was born
You've nourished me and kept me warm
I can't repay the debt I owe
But there are things you ought to know

I've based my life on what you've taught
Though sometimes oh I know we fought
Your faith in God has shown me most
Make room for him and keep him close

The change in life, it comes so fast
That staying close is quite a task
I won't forget your love for me
And how you've raised our family

I'll always be your youngest son
But I'll never be the smallest one
The times we've shared I'll always cherish
My memories will never parish

We move, we grow, in life so fast
I'll cherish all my youthful past
I'll carry on with hopes and fears
Knowing that your prayers are near

My wife and kids, they love you too
For being Granny through and through

So, on we go with life's new treasures
And hope we spend more time together
For God he gave us to each other
And I will always love you Mother

I Called Her Puddles

Rosie's Little Bigmouth was her registered name
Making little puddles was her claim to fame
I loved her when I saw her all crippled on the floor
I just had to stop and buy her at the shopping mall pet store

Full price I had to pay to save her from the strife
Little did I know the impact she would have on my life
Her back leg wasn't straight and a hole on top her head
The Vet he took one look at her and said three days She's dead

I didn't take her back; I couldn't do that to her
She went in shock when we went home, I thought her end was near
She had the strength to pull it out
A glucose shot and baby food was what it was about

She never grew more than four pounds, her hair was not so bright
But she brought me joy, that little dog and would not give up the fight
Through college years a couple jobs, and five US States later
She stayed right by me thick or thin, no one would ever hate her

She listened good and minded well
Loved it all and I could surely tell
Till old did come and slowed her down
The time had come to put her down

I wished her passing in the night
But she would not give up without a fight
The hardest thing I've ever done
To end the life of my little loved one

For thirteen years we enjoyed each other
To this day there has been no other
To her memory I wish to say
I will love her each and every day

Printed in the United States
By Bookmasters